YOU CHOOSE

IMMIGRATING TO AMERICA THROUGH ELLIS ISLAND

A HISTORY-SEEKING ADVENTURE

by Eric Braun

CAPSTONE PRESS
a capstone imprint

Published by Capstone Press, an imprint of Capstone
1710 Roe Crest Drive, North Mankato, Minnesota 56003
capstonepub.com

Library of Congress Cataloging-in-Publication Data
Names: Braun, Eric, 1971– author.
Title: Immigrating to America through Ellis Island : a history-seeking adventure / by Eric Braun.
Description: North Mankato, Minnesota : Capstone Press, 2025. | Series: You choose. Seeking history | Includes bibliographical references. | Audience: Ages 8–12 | Audience: Grades 4–6 | Summary: "YOU are determined to start a new life in America in the early 1900s. But leaving your home in Europe won't be easy. How will you make the long journey across the Atlantic? What will you tell immigration officials when you arrive at Ellis Island? Where will you go if you finally gain entry to the United States? Step back in time to face the challenges real people encountered when they left their homelands and immigrated to America through Ellis Island"—Provided by publisher.
Identifiers: LCCN 2024020621 (print) | LCCN 2024020622 (ebook) ISBN 9781669083412 (hardcover) | ISBN 9781669083382 (paperback) ISBN 9781669083399 (pdf)
Subjects: LCSH: Ellis Island Immigration Station (N.Y. and N.J.)—History—Juvenile literature. | United States—Emigration and immigration—History—Juvenile literature.
Classification: LCC JV6484 .B73 2025 (print) | LCC JV6484 (ebook) | DDC 304.8/73—dc23/eng/20230617
LC record available at https://lccn.loc.gov/2024020621
LC ebook record available at https://lccn.loc.gov/2024020622

Editorial Credits
Editor: Christopher Harbo; Designer: Bobbie Nuytten; Media Researcher: Svetlana Zhurkin; Production Specialist: Whitney Schaefer

Image Credits
Alamy: Contraband Collection, 92, Kirn Vintage Stock, 99, Melissa Jooste, 48; Getty Images: Edwin Levick, 26, 61, Fotosearch, 83, Photos, cover, Topical Press Agency, 21, Transcendental Graphics/Mark Rucker, 86, Universal Images Group/Education Images, 89; Library of Congress: 4, 8, 39, 63, 102; National Park Service: Ellis Island National Monument, 45; The New York Public Library: The Miriam and Ira D. Wallach Division of Art/Prints and Photographs, 11, 58, 103; Shutterstock: Everett Collection, 66, 72, 81, MarinaMonroe, 105, Maya K. Photography, 51; SuperStock: Everett Collection, 18, Image Asset Management, 33

Printed and bound in China. PO 6097

TABLE OF CONTENTS

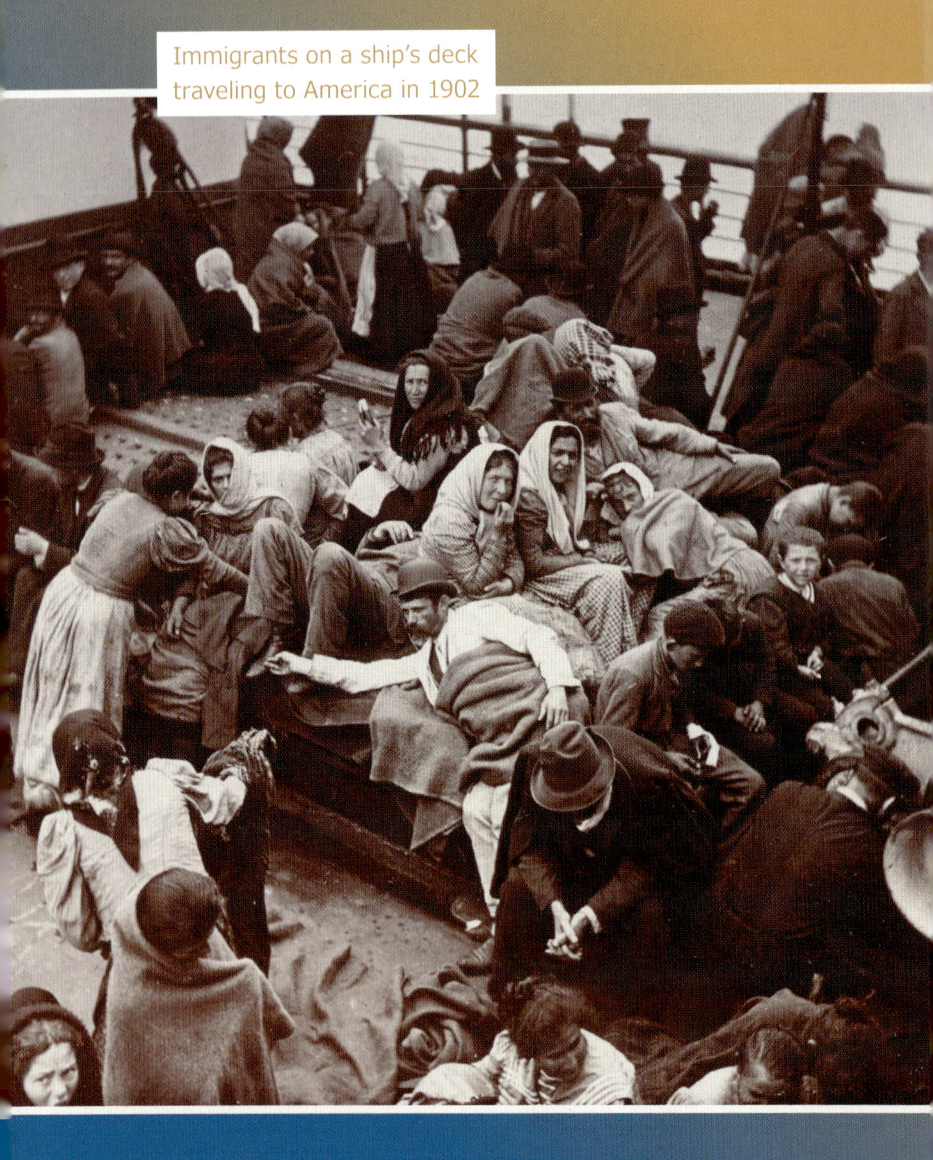
Immigrants on a ship's deck traveling to America in 1902

ABOUT YOUR ADVENTURE

YOU are living in Europe in the early 1900s, and a future in your homeland looks terribly bleak. But you've heard that life in America is much better—and you're determined to go there.

You could be fleeing religious persecution in Russia. Or you may be leaving Bohemia to reunite with family in America. You could be escaping rising nationalism in Germany. Wherever you come from, YOU CHOOSE which path to take. Will you pass through Ellis Island and into the United States? Or, will you be sent back to your homeland?

Turn the page to begin your adventure.

CHAPTER 1

COMING TO AMERICA

You have decided to leave your home in Europe and try to gain entry to the United States. It's the early 1900s, and the world is changing fast. Economic decline and industrialization—the shift from making products by hand to producing them with machines—have made jobs hard to find. As a result, poverty is widespread. And in some countries, nationalism is leading to anger and violence toward minorities and foreigners. Religious persecution, especially of Jewish people, also makes daily life dangerous for many.

Turn the page.

America is not immune to problems. It has gone through economic depression and industrialization too. But the news coming from that country makes it sound like a land of opportunity. More jobs. Religious freedom. A place where you can succeed if you are willing to work hard.

New York City's bustling Broadway in 1906

Indeed, you've heard rumors that everyone in America is rich. One of your friends showed you a photo of his family wearing beautiful clothes and gold jewelry in America. You held that photo for several minutes, examining it carefully. While you don't believe everyone in America is rich, you are sure that life must be better there than it is in Europe. And even though it means leaving the only home you've ever known, you are ready to find out for yourself.

Still, you know leaving won't be easy. Simply traveling from your village to a port city will be challenging. Once there, you'll buy a ticket to sail across the ocean, which will be both expensive and difficult. Then, when you make it to New York, you will be processed by immigration officials and doctors looking for reasons to deny you entry. If you appear sick, mentally unstable, or unable to work, they can send you back home.

Turn the page.

In fact, they can send you home for any reason at all, and that's a scary thought. Many Americans have grown wary of immigrants. They resent newcomers taking jobs that "real" Americans should have. They don't like people from other countries bringing new traditions, new languages, and new cultures to their country. They don't want their lifestyle to change.

Some Americans are also leery of the economic struggles and social tensions in countries like yours. They are afraid immigrants will bring more discord with them. You fear that if you say the wrong thing to an immigration official, you may stoke those fears and be turned away. And even if you get through immigration, you will have to build a new life in a country where some people will hate you just for being an immigrant.

A color postcard from the early 1900s showing Ellis Island

Still, you are optimistic and very excited. The place where you will land in America for processing is called Ellis Island. It is a facility specially built to welcome—or reject—new immigrants. The name—*Ellis Island*—sounds beautiful.

You can't wait to see it.

- To be a Jewish person fleeing religious persecution in Russia, turn to page 13.
- To be a Czech teen hoping to reunite with family in America, turn to page 47.
- To be a German intellectual seeking escape from nationalist violence, turn to page 75.

CHAPTER 2

SEEKING RELIGIOUS FREEDOM

This morning after breakfast, your friend Levi stops at your home with terrible news. Another pogrom has happened in a nearby town. A pogrom is a violent riot in which Jewish people like you are attacked and often killed. They've been happening more often lately.

"I heard it was dozens killed this time," Levi says. "It could be us next!"

That night, you are still thinking about the news. You do not understand why people would want to hurt you just because you are Jewish. You ask your father about it during dinner.

Turn the page.

"Why doesn't the government stop the pogroms?" you ask.

"The government is in on them," your father says sadly. "They want us eliminated."

The words send a chill along your skin.

"Are—are we safe?" your sister, Hannah, asks. She is about to cry.

"Your mother and I have been talking," your father says. "We have decided that it is time for us to leave."

"Where will we go?" you ask.

"America!" your mother says. She gives you and your sister a soft smile. "They have religious freedom there."

Unlike your mother, your father does not smile. "They also have bigots, just like any place," he says. "But it will be better there than here."

Now Hannah does begin to cry. But you are not sad about leaving this life behind. Sure, you will miss friends like Levi. But the Russian government keeps you in deep poverty, and violence is always nearby.

You look at your parents' thin faces in the lamplight. *Yes,* you think. *America is a good idea.*

The first step will be to travel from the western region of the Russian Empire to a coastal city in Germany. Once there, you can book passage to the United States. But you must be careful to avoid Russian patrols. If they catch you, they will put you in prison—if they don't kill you.

You have two options for the first part of your journey. You can try to bribe soldiers for safe passage. Or you can try sneaking away at night.

• To try to bribe your way out, turn to page 16.

• To sneak out on your own, turn to page 18.

Two days later, your uncle comes to dinner. He knows lots of people with political connections, including some you might bribe in the Russian border guard.

As you tend the fireplace, you try to listen in while your father and your uncle talk quietly. Then your father gives your uncle a small satchel of money, and your uncle leaves.

Several nights later, your father makes an announcement. "We will take a walk."

"I'm tired," you say.

"We walk as a family," he replies.

You understand this is important.

The four of you put on your coats and walk down the road. You walk for many blocks until you approach a house on the edge of town. Your father explains that you will meet a man named

Kristoff. Then you will wait for a vehicle to take you across the border and into Germany.

But when you go inside the house, your father is immediately concerned. He looks around the room at four men.

"Where is Kristoff?" he asks.

"Just wait," one of the men says. Two of them snicker.

"This doesn't feel right," your father whispers.

Could your uncle's connection have betrayed him? Is this a trap?

- To trust the men and wait for your ride out of the country, turn to page 21.
- To get out of there, turn to page 23.

You decide to save your money and go it alone. Late one night, the four of you leave home by foot. Your father shoulders a large duffel and has all your family's money sewed into his coat.

You quickly walk out of town and along empty roads. You continue on even after the sun rises, hiding in the trees whenever a cart or vehicle approaches.

An immigrant family with a few belongings packed for their new life in America

Two nights later, you reach a town on the border with Germany. At the edge of town, you approach a small house. Your uncle—who knows many people and has influence—told your father this is a safe house. You knock, and soon the dead bolt clicks and the door swings open.

Inside it is dark. After your eyes adjust, you see a man standing in the room.

"Wait here," he says.

The man goes to a window and looks out. There is a field of tall grass behind the house. Beyond it lies a stand of trees and a rushing river that marks the border with Germany. You also know Russian patrols could be out there.

The man at the window does not light a lamp. He just stares out into the darkness.

"There!" he suddenly whispers, pointing out the window.

Turn the page.

You look out into the woods. At first you see nothing, but then there is a brief flash of light from a lantern. It's a signal. It's time to go.

"Be fast and be silent," the man says.

The four of you slip out a back door and run across the field toward the trees. Your father leads the way, holding Hannah's hand. You and your mother follow. As the trees get closer, you begin to feel a thrill. You're going to make it.

Suddenly, your mother falls. "Oof!" she grunts.

Your father and Hannah don't hear her, and they quickly reach the trees. You look back. Your mother lies on the ground, holding her ankle. You know a Russian patrol could arrive at any second.

"Go on!" your mother whispers. She is clearly in pain and may not be able to walk.

• To help your mother across the field, turn to page 25.
• To wait for your mother in the trees, turn to page 28.

"I don't like this," Hannah whispers.

"This is the plan," you whisper back. "Father and Uncle know what they are doing."

Your parents exchange worried looks. "When will the truck be here?" your father asks.

"Don't worry," says one of the men.

As you wait, your father grows more nervous. Finally, a truck pulls up outside.

A French-made truck on a muddy road in Russia around 1916

Turn the page.

Moments later, the door bursts open. Several men rush in with pistols drawn.

"What is this?" you mother exclaims.

"Shut up!" one of the armed men snaps.

"Wait!" says your father. But the man hits him with the butt of his pistol, and your father collapses.

The men close in on you. You don't know if these are Russian soldiers or simply Russian citizens intent on murdering Jewish people. It doesn't really matter. You and your family have been betrayed, and you know the end is near.

THE END

To follow another path, turn to page 11.
To learn more about immigrating to America through Ellis Island, turn to page 101.

"Okay," your father says to the man. "We will wait."

But when the men are distracted, your father motions toward the door with his eyes. You understand that this means Kristoff is not here and that you need to escape. You squeeze Hannah's hand to signal her to stay close.

Stalling for time, you and your father talk to the men, pretending you trust them. Then you ask for a drink of water. One man goes out to a well. The others are distracted with talk of a soccer game.

Then, suddenly, the four of you bolt out into the street. You stick together, running down one block and then turning into another.

The men chase after you, shouting. But you have a good head start, and soon you make it into the woods. Eventually, you hide behind a large

Turn the page.

fallen log. You stay there until nightfall, and then you continue on.

After a few days, you manage to cross into Germany. You are hungry, tired, and scared. But you are out of Russia.

Eventually, you reach the port town of Bremen. At the docks, you go to the kiosk to buy four tickets on a ship to America. When your father gave your uncle money to bribe the guards, he tried to keep enough to cover the cost of the journey. But now you learn that the price of tickets has gone up. You only have enough money for three tickets, and the ship is boarding now.

"I will stay back," your father says. He turns to you. "Take care of your mother and sister. I will be there soon."

- To buy three tickets and let your father stay back, turn to page 31.
- To stay in Bremen and try to raise money for a fourth ticket, turn to page 33.

You lay down next to your mother in the tall grass. "Keep down," you whisper.

Moments later, a flashlight beam passes over you. A patrol must be passing by! Luckily, the beam of light does not pause. Soon, it goes out. You wait a few minutes to make sure the guards have moved on, and then you help your mother up.

"My ankle is hurt," she says.

"Lean on me," you reply.

The two of you limp through the field to the woods and across the river. Wet and shivering, you reunite with your father and sister.

Safely in Germany, you continue on to the port city of Bremen. Then you buy four tickets on a ship going to America.

About two weeks later, a passenger comes down to the hold with good news. Ellis Island is

Turn the page.

The Statue of Liberty has been welcoming immigrants to America since 1886.

in sight. You and your family climb up onto the deck along with everyone else onboard. Up ahead you see the Statue of Liberty in the harbor. You have heard about this symbol of freedom and equal opportunity. It brings a lump of emotion to your throat.

As the ship slows, another boat comes up alongside it. Some men from that boat board your boat. Passengers line up to talk to one of these immigration officials, and your family does the same. When you reach the front of the line, an official looks you over. Then he says something in English. Another man standing next to him repeats the question in Russian.

"What is your reason for coming to America?" the translator asks.

You remember what your father said about bigots being everywhere. As a Jewish person, you are always wary of discrimination. You know this man could send you back for any reason he wants. You need to be careful how you answer.

- To tell him about the pogroms, turn to page 35.
- To talk about the business your family wants to open, turn to page 37.

Suddenly, you hear footsteps in the distance. A Russian patrol must be approaching! You dash for the trees.

You stay hidden and look back into the field. To your relief, your mother is completely hidden in the tall grass. Meanwhile, Hannah and your father are nowhere to be seen. You know they stuck with the plan—if anyone got separated, they would keep going and meet in Bremen, Germany.

Even so, you decide to wait for your mother. But when the sun rises, you still can't see her in the field. Perhaps she escaped into another part of the woods. Or maybe she turned back.

Reluctantly, you follow the plan and make your way to Bremen. At the port, you find Hannah and your father. Sadly, your mother is not there. You wait a couple days, but she still doesn't show up.

"We have to go home and find her," Hannah cries.

But your father says you can't risk it. You could all be caught and imprisoned, if not killed.

"We all agreed to our plan," your father says. "Your mother is strong. She will find a way to join us on her own."

The next day, you sail for America. Your hearts are heavy, and your sister cries for most of the trip. But during the long journey, you get to know other Jewish people on your ship. In fact, you and your father become very close with a man named Ethan. He plans to join his family in Chicago.

When you reach America, you are all processed through Ellis Island. Soon, you find yourselves standing on the busy streets of New York City.

Turn the page.

"I know you plan to work in New York until you save enough money to open a shoe shop," Ethan says. "But that will take a long time."

"What else can we do?" your father asks.

"My family lives in Chicago," Ethan replies. "They have a music shop and are opening a second location. They need good workers. You could start right away."

Guaranteed work sounds really good, as does having friends in this new land. But you know Chicago is far away. Your mother may not find you when she arrives.

- To go to Chicago with Ethan, turn to page 39.
- To stay in New York, turn to page 41.

You agree that it is best to get at least three of you out while you can. Your father is strong and brave, and you know he will find work here in Bremen. It won't take him long to earn the money to join you.

The voyage across the ocean is sad without your father. But as you get closer to the United States, you feel more optimistic. The facility at Ellis Island is bustling with activity, and you can hear people speaking many different languages. Some people drag large trunks and suitcases, while others have little more than the clothes on their back.

A Russian interpreter is present at your interview with an immigration official. With his help, you are able to pass through.

You have enough money to rent a small boarding room on Orchard Street on the Lower East Side of New York City. You find a

Turn the page.

synagogue to join, and you soon begin making connections with other Jewish people in the neighborhood.

You also find a job in a textile factory, where you cut cloth and assemble garments. The work is grueling, the pay is low, and the conditions are often dangerous. When you finish your shift, you go home to be with Hannah while your mother works in a diner at night.

Meanwhile, you send letters to Bremen, hoping your father will receive them. You tell him you are slowly saving money to open a shoe shop. With any luck, you will have enough by the time he arrives. You just hope he makes it.

THE END

To follow another path, turn to page 11.
To learn more about immigrating to America through Ellis Island, turn to page 101.

Work is not easy to find in Bremen, especially for Jewish people. But your father finally finds a job cleaning out horse stables. Within a few weeks, he manages to save enough money for a fourth ticket. Soon, the four of you are sailing to America together.

When you arrive at Ellis Island, you enter a big hall filled with people. You notice that many

Jewish immigrants from Russia aboard a ship going to America around 1900

Turn the page.

of the immigrants waiting in line are coughing and look very sick. You wonder if they will be turned away.

Up at the front of the line, a young couple is detained and brought to another room out of sight. They were on your ship, and the woman is pregnant. Your heart sinks to think of what may happen to them. Will they be deported? It seems that way.

Just as your worries are at their highest, a man holding a folder approaches your family. He speaks in Russian, saying he can issue your citizenship papers right now for a small fee. That way you can avoid the long line and skip the interview. By now, the idea of the interview is terrifying, so skipping it seems like a great idea. But can you trust this man?

• To take the man up on his offer, turn to page 42.

• To stay in line, turn to page 44.

"We want freedom," you say to the man. "Nothing more than that."

The man writes something on a form, and you keep talking. You tell him about the pogroms. You tell him about living every day in fear under a government that wants to eliminate your people. You tell him about hiding from Russian patrols and sneaking across the border.

"We risked our lives," you say. "We wanted to be in the land of the free."

"Yeah, yeah, yeah," the man says. "Land of the free, beacon of liberty, all that stuff." He stamps your papers and hands them back to you. He looks bored. He must hear stories like yours all day long. To him, the idea of freedom is no big deal. It's just a part of daily life.

"Move along," the man says. "We got a lot of people to help here, in case you didn't notice."

Turn the page.

You look back at all the immigrants behind you, then you look at your family. You almost can't believe it.

"Thank you," you say to the man.

He looks at you with his mouth open, as if he can't believe you're still standing there.

"Get going!" he says. And you do.

THE END

To follow another path, turn to page 11.
To learn more about immigrating to America through Ellis Island, turn to page 101.

Your father tells the man that you and he are skilled cobblers. You intend to open a business selling and repairing shoes.

The man turns and points at Hannah. "What do you do?" he says. "You work?"

Hannah, who is only eight years old, doesn't respond. You can tell she's trying not to cry. It's not fair for this man to single her out like that.

"Can't she talk?" the man asks your mother.

"Say something, honey," your mother says to Hannah. But Hannah can't seem to get anything out. The journey has been difficult, and the intense attention is too much for her.

Now the official calls another worker over. They speak in English, and then the second man pulls Hannah away. He says something to your mother in English, but you don't understand. You don't know what's going on.

Turn the page.

Now the first official stamps your papers and waves you through. You, your father, and mother are admitted to the country. Your mother yells at the man, but he is talking to the next family. Finally, a different official comes over and tells you, in Russian, to wait in a different hall.

After an hour or two, you finally see Hannah walking toward you. She looks calm and is with a woman. The woman explains that because of Hannah's behavior, the officials wanted to examine her mental ability and literacy. Once she settled down, Hannah easily passed the tests.

"I am sorry for all the trouble," the woman says. "But it is over now. Congratulations."

THE END

To follow another path, turn to page 11.
To learn more about immigrating to America through Ellis Island, turn to page 101.

You decide that if your mother can make it to New York, she can also make it to Chicago. You ride a train with Ethan to Chicago, and you meet his family. They are all very kind, and it feels good to have a community to start out with in a new country.

As promised, Ethan's relatives give both you and your father jobs in their music shops. You

Busy State Street in Chicago, Illinois, in the early 1900s

Turn the page.

buy and sell violins, cellos, brass instruments, guitars, and more. Outside of work hours, you begin to practice the guitar. Soon, you can play a few chords and songs.

Meanwhile, your father mails letters to Bremen and to your village in Russia. Sadly, you don't hear anything back. As the months turn into years, you fear that your mother was caught and imprisoned. But your father never gives up hope. He continues to mail her letters every week.

Eventually, you meet someone and begin dating. Soon, you are engaged. You really like this community, and you are forever grateful to Ethan for sharing this opportunity. You only wish your mother could be here for your wedding.

THE END

To follow another path, turn to page 11.
To learn more about immigrating to America through Ellis Island, turn to page 101.

"Thank you, Ethan," your father says. "But we must stay here and wait for my wife."

"Of course," Ethan says. "I wish you luck."

You, your father, and your sister find a synagogue on New York City's Lower East Side. It helps new immigrants find resources. You get clean clothes, blankets, and beds in a large gymnasium where you can stay for a while.

Your father gets a job in a shoe shop. Given his talents as a cobbler, he soon becomes a manager.

You find work building new skyscrapers. Each day, you work high above the city. On your breaks, you stare out over the ocean and think of your mother. You imagine her on a ship just like the one you came over on. You hope it is true.

THE END

To follow another path, turn to page 11.
To learn more about immigrating to America through Ellis Island, turn to page 101.

"Let's do it," you whisper to your father.

He looks uncertain—after all, who can you trust in this new land? But then he looks toward the room where the young couple was taken. He makes up his mind.

"How much?" he says to the man.

The man tells him the price, and your father nods. The man leads you to a corner of the big hall, where you all sit on the floor. He records your names, city of origin, and more on sheets of paper. He asks about your health, and he marks boxes that show you are in good health.

After a few more questions, he pulls a rubber stamp from his coat. He stamps an insignia on the forms and hands them to your father.

"Congratulations," the man says. Then he points to a short line across the hall. "Please proceed to that line over there."

Once again, you find yourself waiting in line. Only now you are less nervous because you believe you're already approved to enter the country.

When you reach the front of the line, your father hands the forms to an official. He takes one look and shakes his head.

"These are fake," the official says in Russian. "What kind of trick are you trying to pull?"

The official calls over some uniformed officers. You are taken to a room and questioned about the papers. The officers accuse you of trying to gain illegal entry to the United States.

Your heart sinks as you realize that you have been tricked into getting yourselves deported.

THE END

To follow another path, turn to page 11.
To learn more about immigrating to America through Ellis Island, turn to page 101.

"No, thank you," your father says to the man.

"Suit yourself," he replies, walking away.

You anxiously wait your turn, watching carefully to see what happens to the immigrants ahead of you. After a while, it becomes clear that almost everyone is getting through without too much trouble. Perhaps the rumors you heard about officials rejecting people for no good reason were just that—rumors.

You think of the couple who was taken to the other room. Are they being deported? If so, perhaps there is a good reason. Perhaps they are spies. Perhaps they have a deadly contagious disease. Who knows?

When it's your turn to be interviewed, all goes smoothly. A doctor checks everyone over and notices that Hannah has a fever. He gives you an address for a synagogue where you can get help finding health services and a place to stay.

Immigration officers processing new arrivals to the United States in the early 1900s

You thank the doctor and board a ferry heading from Ellis Island to New York City. As you stand on the deck, a cool breeze ruffles your hair. You look at your sister, mother, and father. They all are smiling broadly. And so are you.

THE END

To follow another path, turn to page 11.
To learn more about immigrating to America through Ellis Island, turn to page 101.

CHAPTER 3

FOLLOWING FAMILY

You can't remember a time when you didn't dream of going to the United States. It is a favorite topic among your friends in your small village in Bohemia. Even the adults in town speak of it often.

But America's place in your heart is even more special than for most. That's because your father and brother are already living and working there. They left three years ago, when you were 13 years old. Back then, it was too costly to send all four of you.

You can't wait to escape the backbreaking poverty of this village and see them again. But your mother has soured on the idea of going

Turn the page.

to the New World. She has heard rumors that people in America are under strict regulation. Some say that immigrants are enslaved.

"Mama," you say, showing her your father's most recent letter. "Does it sound like he is enslaved? He describes a good life!"

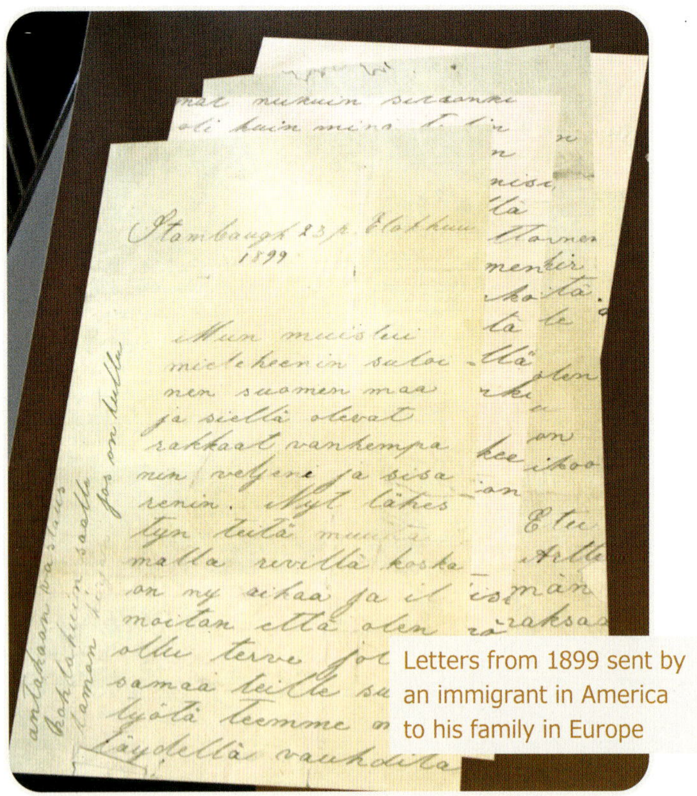

Stambaugh 23 p. Elokuu
1899

Mun muistui
mieleheenin suloi-
nen suomen maa
ja siellä olevat
rakkaat vanhempa
nin veljeni ja sisa
renin. Nyt lähes
tyn teillä muista
malla rivillä koska
on ny aikaa ja il
moitan että olen
ollu terve

Letters from 1899 sent by an immigrant in America to his family in Europe

Your father and brother have settled in St. Louis, Missouri. Your father paints houses, and your brother works in a brewery. They have been sending a little money every few months. You wonder if there is enough to make the trip.

"They are forced to say good things about America," your mother says, echoing the rumors she's heard. "Really, they are enslaved. If we go there, we will be enslaved as well!"

"Okay, Mama," you say. But you don't believe your father and brother would lie about things, even if forced to.

You want to leave—and soon. You want to work a real job, like your brother. Maybe you can get rich! It is a thrilling idea. You go to bed that night and think about what you should do.

• To keep trying to convince your mother, turn to page 50.

• To make a plan to go alone, turn to page 52.

Your friend Michal also has relatives in the United States. He is a little older than you and is the last of his family still living here. Like you, he receives letters from them with money. And like you, Michal is eager to go to America. You invite him over to show his letters to your mother.

"Look, Mama," you say. "Michal's family says they have a better life too. You were friends with his mother and father. They wouldn't lie."

"These are not their voices," she says, pointing at Michal's letters. "These are not real."

"I believe they are real," Michal says. "My parents say things that only they would know."

"Have a kolach," your mother says, trying to change the subject. She slides a plate of the traditional Czech pastries toward him.

You think of your father. He always said your mother made the best kolaches in all the land.

Czech kolaches

The three of you sit in silence for a few moments eating. Your mother looks very sad and worried, as if something else is on her mind. You sense that you have one more chance to convince her.

Maybe you just need to talk to her some more. If something is bothering her, maybe you can help. On the other hand, you may need to find a way to prove your father is telling the truth about America—something she can't deny. Looking at the kolaches, an idea begins to form.

- To ask her what's really the matter, turn to page 53.
- To try your plan, turn to page 55.

You know your mother won't change her mind. You also know she won't want you to leave her—so you must plan your trip in secret.

One day, your friend Michal has you over for tea. His family in America has been sending him money, and now he is ready to make the trip himself. When he invites you to travel with him, you're tempted. He's a little older than you, and it would be great to travel together. You would have someone to rely on if anything went wrong.

However, Michal is ready to leave very soon. Trouble is, you do not have money of your own, and your mother surely would not share.

"I'll share with you," Michal says. "We'll have to buy cheap tickets, but I think we can do it."

He *thinks* you can do it. Is that enough?

- To stay back and find a way to save your own money, turn to page 57.
- To go with Michal, turn to page 60.

After Michal leaves, you and your mother sit at the table again.

"Mama," you say, taking her hand. "You seem worried. What is it?"

"It's . . . ," she begins, but then pauses. "It's my eyes. My vision is failing."

"You seem fine," you say.

"It's easy at home," she says. "I know home by memory. Traveling would be hard."

For the first time you notice that she doesn't quite focus on you when she speaks. You can see that she is truly scared.

"I will take care of you," you say. "I promise. Let's go see Dad and Jacob."

In the end, she agrees to go. You travel by cart to Antwerp, Belgium, where you board a ship. On the voyage, you help your mother get around.

Turn the page.

When you finally arrive at Ellis Island, you follow the crowd through the great hall. Soon, you reach the front of a line where an immigration official who speaks Czech questions you. You answer his questions, and he passes you along to be examined by a doctor.

The doctor speaks English as he examines you and your mother. When he gives her a brief vision test, she doesn't do well. With a piece of white chalk, he writes an English word on the back of her dress. Then he points you toward another station.

Your mother starts to panic. "They're going to send us home!" she says.

You have heard rumors that only healthy, fit immigrants are allowed into the country. Perhaps your mother's poor vision will cost you entry.

- To go quietly along, turn to page 62.
- To appeal to an officer for help, turn to page 64.

"I have an idea, Mama," you say. "Write a letter to Papa asking about the kolaches in America. If he is being forced to say good things, he will say the kolaches there are the best. If he is speaking for himself, he will say your kolaches are better."

To your surprise, your mother agrees. You send the letter the next day.

Several weeks later, you get his reply.

"A bakery here makes something similar to kolaches," he writes. "Sadly, they are nothing like yours, my dear. They only make me miss you more."

Tears well up in your mother's eyes. The letter has done the trick—she wants to go to America.

Your father has been sending money home with most of his letters. After adding up what

Turn the page.

your mother has socked away, you decide you have enough to go now.

You send a letter to your father telling him you are on your way. Then you travel to the German port city of Cuxhaven.

Now it's time to buy your tickets to sail to America. You can spend most of your money on first-class tickets. You'll get to ride upstairs and eat better food. Or you can save money by getting tickets to ride below deck in steerage. It will be a more difficult journey, but you will have more money left over for the trip from New York to St. Louis.

- To sail first class, turn to page 66.
- To sail in steerage, turn to page 68.

While you appreciate Michal's offer, it doesn't seem fair to take his money. Also, you don't want to arrive broke in America. No, you prefer to do this on your own.

The next time your mother sends you to the market to buy food, you pocket some of the change. It's a small amount, but it's a start. The next time you go, you do the same thing. It takes more than a year, but finally you save enough to make the trip to New York.

One morning, you stash all your money in a coat pocket and give your mother a big hug. She thinks you're going to the market. Instead, you make the long journey to a port and buy a ticket to America.

When you arrive at Ellis Island a few weeks later, the processing facility is swarming with activity. Different people are saying different things in different languages. It's confusing, and

Turn the page.

Hundreds of immigrants waiting to be processed in the Registry Room on Ellis Island

you don't know what to do. So, you simply follow the crowd.

Finally, you hear someone speaking Czech. You follow the voice and wait in this man's line. When you get to him, he says, "Papers?"

You hand him your immigration papers, and he asks a few questions. Before you know it, you are standing on a busy street corner in New York City. In that moment, you really miss your mother.

Soon, you find a community of Eastern Europeans on the Lower East Side. After settling in, you send a telegram to your father and find a job collecting trash. After work you hang out in a café where you meet other young Eastern Europeans like yourself. You quickly make friends.

Eventually, you hear back from your father. He says he will wire you money for a train ticket. While you are sad to leave your new friends, you can't wait to see your father and brother again. Together, perhaps you can convince your mother to come to America.

THE END

To follow another path, turn to page 11.
To learn more about immigrating to America through Ellis Island, turn to page 101.

Because Michal is older and has money, you like the idea of traveling with him. You think it will be easier and less lonely than going alone.

One morning, you tell your mother you are leaving for America with Michal. When she gets upset, you ask once more if she would join you. But she won't change her mind—she is staying. So, with a weight in your heart, you leave her.

The sea voyage to America is difficult. Both you and Michal get seasick, but you remain very excited. You talk with others on the ship, sharing your hopes and fears. Some talk about the new immigration laws the United States has passed. Newcomers can be turned away if they aren't healthy, can't work, or aren't literate in at least one language.

One man, who wears a plaid wool jacket, says, "They don't need a reason. You can be turned away for anything at all."

Excited immigrants waving to the Statue of Liberty in 1915

By the time you approach Ellis Island, you're really worried about getting through. As you pass the Statue of Liberty in the harbor, the man in the plaid jacket walks up to you and Michal.

"Listen," the man says. "My cousin is an immigration officer on that island. For a small fee, I'll make sure he passes you, no questions asked."

- To take the man up on his offer, turn to page 70.
- To save your money and take your chances going through immigration, turn to page 72.

"Try to relax," you say to your mother. "Let's show them we can follow the rules."

Your mother has trouble settling down, though. Due to her poor eyesight, she can't see where you are going. As you lead her along, she gets bumped and jostled. Then you reach a second doctor who gives her a more thorough eye exam.

After she gets a few answers wrong, she yells, "Leave me alone!"

Your mother continues yelling and flailing her arms. You know she is scared and confused, but the doctor gets angry. Suddenly, your mother is led into a small room without you. The doctor tells you to proceed to the end of processing. After you pass, you find the doctor and ask about your mother.

The doctor shakes his head. "I suspect she'll be going home," he says.

European women going through a physical examination at Ellis Island around 1910

You wait outside the door for the longest time, hoping your mother will come out. You try to understand what happened. Is she being turned away because of her eyesight? Is it because she yelled at the doctor?

Soon, a police officer forces you to leave. You realize that you have made it to America, but your mother has not. You think of her sailing home alone and scared—and your heart sinks.

THE END

To follow another path, turn to page 11.
To learn more about immigrating to America through Ellis Island, turn to page 101.

You pull your mother back to the official who spoke Czech. He is talking to a family and is annoyed to be interrupted. But you show him the writing on your mother's back anyway.

"What is this?" you ask.

"It says vision," he says. "She will be tested and may be turned away." Then he whispers, "Just put your arm around her as if you are comforting her. Then casually wipe off the chalk. When you bring her to the next station, act as if nobody ever put chalk on her."

You follow the official's instructions and proceed toward the final check station. Surprisingly, you are processed through the gate within minutes.

Once in New York, you find a train station and buy two tickets. When you finally arrive in St. Louis, you look up your father and brother's address. Your stomach tingles with excitement as you knock on their apartment door.

When the door swings open, you see your brother and yell out his name. He hollers in excitement, and your father comes rushing over. He looks strong and healthy. It is clear, even to your mother, that he and your brother are free here. They are not regulated or enslaved.

That night, you all have dinner together. You tell the story of the kind official who spoke Czech at Ellis Island. Your father raises his glass in a toast.

"Cheers to him," he says.

THE END

To follow another path, turn to page 11.
To learn more about immigrating to America through Ellis Island, turn to page 101.

You decide to buy first-class tickets because the conditions in steerage are crude. The rocking of the boat is more intense down there, leading to sea sickness for many. Besides that, being packed in such tight quarters can spread disease. You want your mother's trip to be as easy and healthy as possible.

When you arrive at Ellis Island, you see passengers from steerage coming up. Many look

European immigrants and their luggage aboard a ship arriving in New York City in 1913

very ill and smell of vomit and diarrhea. A few of them are still throwing up.

You are glad you decided to go first class, even though you are nearly broke now. At least you made it without getting sick. And that is important—you realize—when you get checked out by a doctor. You learn those who are sick can be detained, quarantined, or even sent back home.

But you and your mother pass your check-ups, and soon you are in New York City.

You are anxious to get to St. Louis. But you spent so much money on your journey here that you don't have enough for train tickets. You will have to find jobs here, as well as a place to live. Although you have virtually nothing, you are confident you will be okay.

THE END

To follow another path, turn to page 11.
To learn more about immigrating to America through Ellis Island, turn to page 101.

You decide to save money and buy the cheap tickets. But halfway through the voyage, you regret your choice. Seasick people vomit all around you, and the bathrooms are backed up with filth. Although you and your mother find a spot next to a kind family, their baby develops a high fever and a spotty rash.

By the time you reach Ellis Island, you don't feel well. One minute you have the chills, the next you are burning up. A doctor diagnoses you with measles and sends you to the Ellis Island Immigrant Hospital on a separate island.

At the hospital, you are examined by more doctors. Then you are given shots and other medicines. On top of being scared and delirious with fever, you don't know where your mother is.

But after a while, you begin to recover. You ask about your mother again and again, but nobody has any information.

A little over a week later, you are released from the hospital and ferried to New York City. You walk off the dock and sit on a bench. Your mother had all your money. You have no job, no friends, no family.

Then you see a familiar figure walking toward the ferry dock. It is your mother!

"Mama! Is that really you?" you call out.

She turns toward you and smiles. You run to her, and you embrace.

"Every day I waited here," she says. "I watched and I waited. I knew you would come."

THE END

To follow another path, turn to page 11.
To learn more about immigrating to America through Ellis Island, turn to page 101.

"Let's do it," you say to Michal. "We shouldn't take any chances."

Michal doesn't look so sure, but in the end he agrees.

You ask the man his price. Although it costs almost all you have left, you pay him. When you get off the boat, you follow the man toward Ellis Island's processing area. He walks quickly and starts to pull away. Suddenly, you can't see him anymore.

"He's gone!" you say.

"I knew it!" Michal says.

You feel guilty for pushing this idea on him. But it's too late now.

As you pass through the processing area, you worry about being rejected because you are broke and may become a burden on society. But you and Michal convince immigration officials you are hard workers, and they let you through.

Now you are glad you traveled to New York City with Michal. Although you are penniless, he has family living in a community of Central and Eastern Europeans. You decide to stay with them until you can be reunited with your father and brother.

In the meantime, Michal's family is kind to you. Their house smells like the foods your mother makes back home. It is a nice memory. But without your own family, it is also a sad one.

THE END

To follow another path, turn to page 11.
To learn more about immigrating to America through Ellis Island, turn to page 101.

You tell the man no. He immediately goes off to sell his idea to someone else.

"He was trying to hustle us," Michal says.

Clearly, you must keep your wits about you here. Con men are looking to take advantage of immigrants like yourselves.

On Ellis Island, the line to get through immigration is long. The process takes most of the day, but in the end you get through quite easily.

Immigrants going through the checkpoint before being admitted to the United States

That evening, you arrive at Michal's family's apartment. Everyone cries when Michal walks in. It is a sweet scene, but it also breaks your heart. You wish your mother was here.

Michal's parents loan you money for a train ticket. Soon, you are zipping across the countryside toward St. Louis.

When you arrive, your father and brother are waiting for you at the station. Instantly, you are overcome with emotion. You hadn't realized how much you missed them until now. Sadly, you know you will soon miss your mother just as much.

The next day, you begin sending letters telling her how great it is here. You just hope she believes you and will come.

THE END

To follow another path, turn to page 11.
To learn more about immigrating to America through Ellis Island, turn to page 101.

CHAPTER 4

FLEEING RISING NATIONALISM

Though the Great War ended nearly two years ago, life in Germany is anything but peaceful. A revolution in Russia has kicked off the rise of Communism—a political movement centered on the idea that all property should be publicly owned. Communists believe that power should lie with the workers, and government and business owners should have limited power. But to gain that power, Communists believe workers must rise up in protest.

This belief has created a fear of Communism in countries all over the world, including the United States and your homeland of Germany.

Turn the page.

Germany has seen some Communist uprisings, but they have not gained much of a following. Instead, a backlash of nationalism has been growing. These nationalists believe that criticizing the government is unpatriotic. They also believe in using violence and war to keep social order.

The nationalist movement is upsetting. You are a professor and a pacifist who believes war is always wrong. And although you are not a Communist, you do have sympathy for the Communist movement. You agree that workers create value and therefore should have power, though you are careful never to speak of your agreement out loud.

Paramilitary groups patrol the streets of your city. An academic friend of yours was even attacked by one of these groups recently. And you're not sure, but are you secretly being watched? Why does that military truck park near your home so often?

You don't know what's going to happen, but you're certain you must get your wife and toddler out of Germany. So, one morning, you secretly gather food and clothing and get on a train with your family. You are going to America, where you believe you can feel safe and free. You speak a little English, which you hope will help you fit in.

That afternoon you arrive at the port. There is a ship leaving in an hour, but it is overcrowded and there are no beds. You will be sleeping on the floor in steerage. You want to leave as soon as possible, but you also want your family to be comfortable.

- To get on the ship leaving today, turn to page 78.
- To try for a less crowded ship leaving in two days, turn to page 79.

You don't want to wait, so you buy tickets for your family to leave today. On the boat, you ride in steerage. This space below deck is crowded and poorly ventilated. The ship is large, but even so it is tossed by the wind and waves. Many passengers get seasick, including you and your toddler, Annika.

Every day you wait in line for your food, but you and Annika keep throwing up. You're not the only ones. Soon, the smell of vomit is everywhere, and that makes it even harder to keep food down. You also notice that some of the passengers have a red rash that looks like measles.

By the end of the first week, you are doing better. But Annika is sicker than ever. She is thin, listless, and shivering.

"Do something!" your wife implores.

- To take Annika up on deck to get fresh air, turn to page 81.
- To wrap her in an extra blanket, turn to page 83.

You know the voyage lasts two weeks, so you decide to wait two days for a less crowded ship. And you're glad you do.

During the trip, several passengers get sick. Because the ship is a bit less crowded, you're able to spread out and keep your distance. When you finally reach New York, everyone in your family seems healthy.

You and your family are standing on deck when the Statue of Liberty comes into view. Your skin tingles at the sight of this symbol of freedom. As you understand it, people in America are free to have differing political views. They also aren't attacked or jailed for their beliefs.

The ship drops anchor in the harbor, and a barge pulls alongside it. You thought you would be processed on Ellis Island, but instead you are directed onto the barge, where a doctor checks

Turn the page.

you over. Thankfully, the three of you pass the checkup easily. Next, you must talk with an immigration official. He looks over your papers, and then he glances at you and says something in English.

"Why are you here?" an interpreter says in German.

Suddenly, you remember how people in your country are so often persecuted, even killed, for voicing the wrong beliefs. Things are supposed to be better here, but are they?

- To say you want to seek your fortune, turn to page 85.
- To admit you don't feel safe in Germany because of your views, turn to page 87.

You carry your sick daughter through the crowd. She is shivering, but her skin feels hot with fever.

You climb the stairs, and soon you are out on the deck. The cool, fresh air smells a lot better than the rancid air below deck. Also, you don't feel the boat rocking as much here.

Steerage passengers sleeping and passing time on deck in the early 1900s

Turn the page.

Almost instantly, Annika relaxes in your arms. Soon, she is sleeping.

After a couple hours Annika stirs and smiles at you. You smile back, but then you see a rash on her neck. Could this be measles? You stay up on deck as much as possible during the final two days of the voyage, avoiding the crowd and smell down below.

Finally, you arrive in New York. You carry Annika onto a barge where your family will be checked out by a doctor. If they think Annika is sick, they may separate you or send your family back to Germany. Do you ask for help or pretend everything is fine in the hope of getting into America?

- To ask for help, turn to page 90.
- To pretend she is fine, turn to page 92.

Annika says she is freezing, so you wrap a second blanket around her. Her body stiffens and she retches, but there is nothing left in her stomach. You rock her gently, and soon she settles down. Eventually, you both fall asleep.

The ship's steerage was designated for cargo and passengers who couldn't afford a private cabin.

Turn the page.

When you awake, Annika's skin is very clammy, and her face is burning hot.

"Ani," you whisper, shaking her gently. "Wake up."

Your wife wakes up and feels Annika's skin. "We need a doctor," she says.

You keep trying to revive Annika while your wife looks for help. But your daughter is barely breathing now. You begin to shout her name and shake her harder, but nothing works. By morning, she is no longer breathing at all.

When you dock at Ellis Island, you carry her body off the ship. You are so sad that you don't even care if they let you into America.

THE END

To follow another path, turn to page 11.
To learn more about immigrating to America through Ellis Island, turn to page 101.

"Money," you say to the man in English. "I will get rich here."

The man smiles and says something back. Because he speaks quickly—and your English is limited—you don't understand. Still, he allows you and your family into the country.

Life is not easy in New York. Your family finds a room in a ramshackle boarding house. But the only job you can get is cleaning filthy bathrooms in the train station.

You also discover that many Americans react with bitterness or anger toward Germans. And because of anti-German feelings, many schools have stopped teaching German. So, when you spot an ad for a German teacher at a private high school, you can't believe your luck.

You apply for the job and are hired. Before your first day, a friend at your boarding house

Turn the page.

People watching the New York Giants play at the Polo Grounds in 1921

tells you about a job as an usher at the Polo Grounds. It's a baseball park where the New York Giants play.

Baseball is the American pastime. Working at the ballpark might be a great way to fit into American society. But it requires a long subway ride to and from work every day, whereas the high school is nearby. Both jobs offer similar pay.

- To teach high school German, turn to page 94.
- To work at the ballpark, turn to page 95.

"Germany is not safe for people like me," you say sadly.

"People like you?" he asks.

"I believe in workers' rights, better working conditions, fair wages," you say. "That does not fit well with much of the thinking in my country right now."

The official says something to the interpreter. The interpreter turns to you.

"Are you a Communist?" he asks.

"No," you reply. He asks how you feel about capitalism. You are suspicious of capitalism, certainly. But you simply say, "I am excited to learn about it."

The official passes you. That night, you take your family out to a New York café for dinner. While you eat and talk, another customer stops

Turn the page.

at your table. He picks up a water glass, yells something in English, and empties the water in your lap. Then he walks out.

Your daughter begins to cry. "It's nothing," you say, trying to comfort her.

You are about to leave when another man approaches. You get ready for a second attack, but instead he speaks in German.

"It's okay," he says. "I am German too."

You invite him to sit with you.

"Many Americans have anti-German feelings," he explains. "But I'm told some places are better than others. I am on my way to Milwaukee, Wisconsin. Many Germans live there. You should go there as well."

You thank him for the advice.

Downtown Milwaukee, Wisconsin, around 1920

That night, you and your wife talk. It would be costly to travel all the way to Milwaukee. On the other hand, life sounds better there than here in New York.

- To stay in New York, turn to page 96.
- To go to Milwaukee, turn to page 98.

You'll gladly go back to Germany if it means saving Annika, so you tell the doctor everything. He doesn't speak German, but he gets the idea and takes her temperature. He looks alarmed at the result and calls for help.

Two nurses come over, and one of them picks up Annika. Then they rush to a different room.

Your wife screams, but the nurses keep going. The doctor tries to keep you both calm, but you don't understand what's going on. Finally, another man approaches.

"They are going to take care of your child," he says in German. "You must continue through immigration now. Come with me to process your papers."

You do as you are told. The man asks you a few questions, but it's hard to concentrate because you're so worried about Annika.

When you finish, they send you to a detention center to wait. There, you learn that Annika has measles and is being quarantined in a hospital.

After several long days, a nurse comes in with Annika. Your daughter is walking and looks healthy. You cry in relief and hug her.

You are in America, you are healthy, and you are together. Whatever happens next, you know you can handle it.

THE END

To follow another path, turn to page 11.
To learn more about immigrating to America through Ellis Island, turn to page 101.

"Ani, you must stop your crying and moaning," you say to her. "The Americans will not want you to bring disease into their country."

You carry your daughter through the lines. When you reach the doctor, he takes a long look at the child lying limp in your arms.

"Can she walk?" he asks.

"Of course," you answer. "But she is sleeping now."

"Wake her up," the doctor says.

The East-Asiatic Company, Limited.
BALTIC AMERICA LINE.

INSPECTION CARD

(Immigrants and Steerage Passengers).

Port of departure, DANZIG.
Name of ship, S. S. Estonia
Name of Immigrant, Jzacki, Jan
Date of departure,
Last residence, Poland

Inspected and passed at DANZIG.
UNITED STATES PUBLIC HEALTH SERVICE
Seal Stamp of Consular or Medical Officer

Passed at quarantine, port of U. S.
(Date).

SENT TO HOSPITAL DEC 4 1925

Passed by Immigration Bureau port of
(Date).

(The following to be filled in by ship's surgeon or agent prior to or after embarcation).
Ship's list or manifest 10 No. on ship's list or manifest 15

Berth No. | Steamship inspection | 1st day. 1 2 3 4 5 6 7 8 9 10 11 12 13 14 15 16 17 18 19

An inspection card from 1925 with a stamp directing an immigrant to the hospital

You do as you are told and set Annika on the floor. She wobbles and leans against her mother.

"She doesn't look good," the doctor says.

"Just tired," you say, picking her up. The man waves you through.

Once you are in New York, a feeling of panic sets in. Your baby's fever is back, and you are in a strange new country. You hope you can find health care somewhere, and fast. Your child's life depends on it.

THE END

To follow another path, turn to page 11.
To learn more about immigrating to America through Ellis Island, turn to page 101.

You have always been a teacher—so you take the job in the high school. It feels good to use your true skills. Soon, your family moves into an apartment building where several other German families live. You make friends, and life seems good.

But the school receives complaints for teaching German. Some families threaten to pull their children out of the school if it doesn't drop the program.

At the end of the school year, you receive some bad news. The school is canceling the German program. No reasons are given, but it doesn't really matter. For now, you'll be back to cleaning bathrooms in the train station.

THE END

To follow another path, turn to page 11.
To learn more about immigrating to America through Ellis Island, turn to page 101.

You came to America to start a new life. Why not start a new career too? Working in a ballpark sounds exciting.

Every day, you take the long subway ride to the Polo Grounds in Upper Manhattan. You use the time to read books in English. You also listen to people talking in the subway cars. In this way, you learn the language and how to fit in as an American.

You also enjoy working in the ballpark. It is a beautiful place, and you learn to love baseball. You think less and less about politics or your homeland. You truly think of yourself as an American.

THE END

To follow another path, turn to page 11.
To learn more about immigrating to America through Ellis Island, turn to page 101.

"Let's stay here for a while," you say. "It's a big city with lots of opportunities."

Your wife agrees, and the next day you set out to find work. But every employer you talk to turns you away when they hear your German accent.

You soon learn about a growing demand for auto mechanics. You have always been a fast learner, so you check out library books about engine mechanics. Eventually, you find a job as an assistant in a garage. In time, you are promoted to full mechanic.

Almost every day you face some cruel comment, and sometimes you fear for your safety. When Annika starts school, she makes friends, but she also faces bullying. Students call her anti-German slurs, and one boy pulls her hair every day.

Meanwhile, back in Germany, the fascists have gained control of the government. This leads to even more intense fear of Germans among Americans.

One night, you are jumped and beat up after work. It hurts, but not nearly as much as watching the Nazi party take over your home country. You fear that another world war is coming and the anti-German bigotry you face will probably get worse.

THE END

To follow another path, turn to page 11.
To learn more about immigrating to America through Ellis Island, turn to page 101.

"I don't like it here," your wife says. You know she is thinking of the man who poured water on you in the café. You agree to leave New York.

The train ride across the country is beautiful. When you reach Milwaukee, you settle into a German neighborhood and quickly make friends. You get a job as a machinist. You shape metal for various purposes. The pay is good, and you enjoy working with your hands.

As the years go by, the news from Germany changes. The Nazi party is in charge, and they have invaded Poland. Soon, another Great War begins. The United States hasn't joined the fight, but you don't know how long they will stay out of it. If the fascists win, it would be very bad for people everywhere. America will surely do what it must to prevent that from happening.

Workers at a Milwaukee, Wisconsin, machinery factory around 1930

Sure enough, you eventually begin working on new types of metal sheets. They are parts for warplanes and other military vehicles. Very soon, your new country will be at war with your old one.

THE END

To follow another path, turn to page 11.
To learn more about immigrating to America through Ellis Island, turn to page 101.

CHAPTER 5

GATEWAY TO LIBERTY

Toward the end of the 1800s, the United States needed a more organized system to handle its rising immigration rates. In 1891, the Immigration Act was passed. It established new procedures for inspecting and processing immigrants. In 1892, Ellis Island opened in New York Harbor. It became a primary point of entry for many immigrants coming to America.

At that time, immigrants came to the United States for many reasons. Communities throughout Europe suffered deep poverty, while America had a more promising economy.

European immigrants getting off the boat in 1920

Many people also sought to escape political unrest in their home countries or to pursue religious freedom.

Jewish people, in particular, faced widespread oppression. In Russia, which had a large Jewish population, persecution was especially bad. Violent attacks—called pogroms—often targeted Jewish communities.

The hope for a better life motivated many Jewish people and other immigrants to cross the Atlantic. Some traveled as a family. Others came alone, hoping to earn enough money to bring family members over later.

Upon arrival at Ellis Island, immigrants underwent a thorough inspection and screening process. Medical examinations screened for

An immigration officer conducting a health check of a mother with three children in the early 1900s

contagious diseases. Legal inspections made sure people had proper documentation, didn't have violent criminal backgrounds, and didn't have subversive political agendas. Inspectors also tried to determine if immigrants would be able to support themselves without public assistance.

After they were processed, immigrants faced an uncertain welcome from their new neighbors. While some Americans welcomed newcomers, others feared and rejected them. Anti-immigrant sentiment, especially against Germans, increased after the United States joined World War I (1914–1918) in 1917. As a result, many immigrants found safety by living in communities of people from their own home country or region.

In the 1920s, new laws began limiting immigration and the countries people could come from. With the smaller numbers arriving, immigrants were processed on the ships, and Ellis Island became mainly a holding area.

In 1954, Ellis Island officially closed. Today, its legacy endures as the National Museum of Immigration. As a museum, it offers visitors insights into the challenges faced by those seeking a new life in the United States. It also serves as an important reminder of the nation's immigrant roots.

Visitors in the Registry Room of the Ellis Island National Museum of Immigration

Ellis Island Timeline

1775: New York merchant Samuel Ellis purchases the island.

1808: New York state buys the island, and the U.S. government begins renting it to use for military purposes.

1890: The U.S. government orders the U.S. Navy to remove explosives from the island and provides money to begin building up facilities to process immigrants.

1892: On January 1, Ellis Island officially opens as an immigration processing center; more than 400,000 immigrants are processed there in its first year.

1905–1906: A second island is built up to hold a contagious disease ward.

1917: The United States enters World War I. Immigrants from enemy countries are detained at Ellis Island.

1919: Following World War I and the Russian Revolution, a fear of Communism spreads to America; immigrants considered to be subversive are detained at Ellis Island and often deported.

1921: The Emergency Quota Act is enacted, limiting the number of immigrants allowed into the country.

1924: The National Origins Act is passed, which puts even stricter limits on immigration; immigrants now must get visas in American consulates before leaving for America; this leads to a dramatic drop in immigration numbers.

1950: The Internal Security Act is passed, explicitly prohibiting immigrants with previous links to Communist and fascist organizations.

1954: Ellis Island closes as an immigration processing facility in November.

1965: Ellis Island becomes a part of the Statue of Liberty National Monument, which puts the National Park Service in charge of the facility; that same year, the Immigration and Naturalization Act ends the earlier quota system based on national origin.

1976–1984: Ellis Island is opened to the public for tours.

1990: After restorations, the main building on Ellis Island opens again to the public as a museum devoted to the immigrant experience.

2001: The American Family Immigration History Center opens, allowing visitors (and visitors to its website) to explore a huge collection of passenger records.

Other Paths to Explore

1. Many immigrants left their families behind until they earned enough money in the United States to send for them. What would it be like to be on your own in a new country with your family back in your home country? Would you rather be the person who goes to America alone or stays back and waits? Why?

2. Immigration officials on Ellis Island had a lot of power to help new arrivals or to make things difficult for them. If you were one of those officials, what are some things you could have done to help immigrants?

3. Imagine you are a child who arrives at Ellis Island sick, and you are separated from your family. How would it feel to be without your family in a hospital where everyone around you speaks English, a language you do not understand?

Bibliography

Bayor, Ronald H. *Encountering Ellis Island.* Johns Hopkins University Press, 2014.

History.com: Ellis Island
history.com/topics/immigration/ellis-island

National Park Service: Ellis Island
nps.gov/elis/index.htm

PBS American Experience: Immigration and Deportation at Ellis Island
pbs.org/wgbh/americanexperience/features/goldman-immigration-and-deportation-ellis-island

Statue of Liberty, Ellis Island Foundation, Inc.: Ellis Island
statueofliberty.org/ellis-island

Statue of Liberty, Ellis Island Foundation, Inc.: Ellis Island Overview & History
statueofliberty.org/ellis-island/overview-history

Szejnert, Malgorzata. *Ellis Island: A People's History.* Scribe Publications, 2009. English translation 2020 (Scribe).

Glossary

bigot (BIG-uht)—a person who treats people of another race with hatred

Communism (KAHM-yuh-ni-zuhm)—a way of organizing a country so that all the land, houses, and factories belong to the government, and the profits are shared by all

deport (di-PORT)—to send people back to their own country

fascism (FASH-iz-uhm)—a form of government in which a dictator and the dictator's political party have complete control over a country

industrialization (in-duhss-tree-uh-lye-ZAY-shuhn)—the widespread development of businesses and factories in a region or country

nationalism (NASH-uh-nuh-liz-uhm)—pride and love of one's native country that emphasizes the promotion of its culture and interests above those of other nations

persecution (pur-suh-KYOO-shuhn)—cruel or unfair treatment, often because of race or religious beliefs

pogrom (POH-gruhm)—an organized attack against a minority group, particularly Jewish people

quarantine (KWOR-uhn-teen)—to keep a person, animal, or plant away from others to stop a disease from spreading

synagogue (SIN-a-gog)—a building where Jewish people come together to pray

Read More

Forest, Christopher. *Immigration Through Ellis Island.* Minneapolis: Pogo, 2021.

Levy, Janey. *Ellis Island.* Buffalo, NY: Gareth Stevens Publishing, 2025.

Spengler, Kremena. *The Immigrant Experience.* Mankato, MN: Creative Education, 2025.

Internet Sites

Britannica Kids: Ellis Island
kids.britannica.com/kids/article/Ellis-Island/399857

Kiddle: Ellis Island Facts for Kids
kids.kiddle.co/Ellis_Island

Kids Discover: Ellis Island
online.kidsdiscover.com/unit/ellis-island

JOIN OTHER HISTORICAL ADVENTURES WITH MORE YOU CHOOSE SEEKING HISTORY!

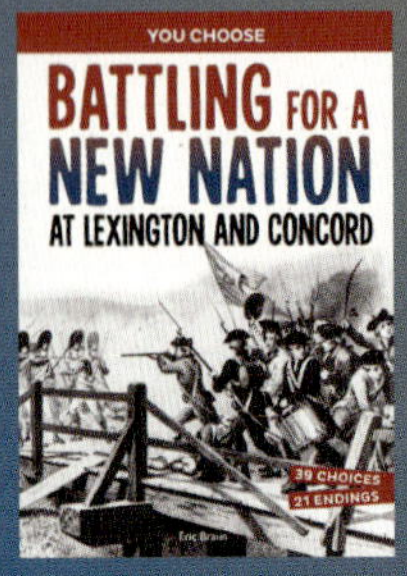

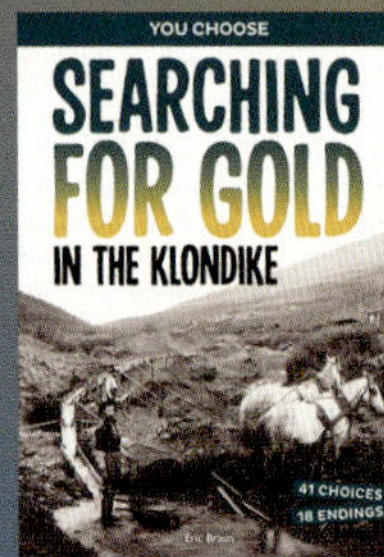

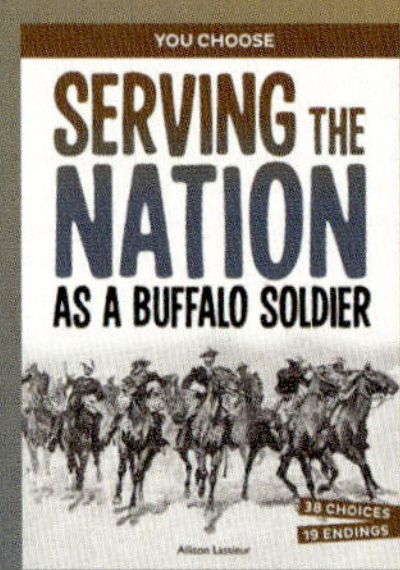

About the Author

photo by Jeff Wheeler

Eric Braun is a children's author and editor. He has written dozens of books on many topics, and one of his books was read by an astronaut on the International Space Station for kids on Earth to watch. Eric lives in Minneapolis, Minnesota, with his wife, two kids, and a dog who is afraid of cardboard.